The Knight Watchmen

Copyright © Mainframe Joint Venture 1994
Licensed by Copyright Promotions Ltd

Published by Hodder Children's Books 1995

10 9 8 7 6 5 4 3 2 1

All rights reserved. No part of this publication may be reproduced, stored in a retrieval system, or transmitted, in any form or by any means, without the prior written permission of the publisher, nor be otherwise circulated in any form of binding or cover other than that in which it is published and without a similar condition being imposed on the
subsequent purchaser.

ISBN 0 340 63628 9

Printed and bound in Great Britain by Cox and Wyman Ltd,
Reading, Berkshire

Hodder Children's Books
A division of Hodder Headline plc
338 Euston Road
London NW1 3BH

The Knight Watchmen

Dave Morris

Hodder Children's Books

ESSEX COUNTY LIBRARY

Introduction

This is a REBOOT adventure gamebook. A gamebook gives you the chance to decide how the story will go. You start at page 1 just as you would with a normal book - but you can enjoy a gamebook over and over again, with a different adventure each time.

You will need a die. Also have a pencil to hand, to record access codes and Game stars on the adventure notes pages at the back of the book. Access codes appear when you have discovered a useful item or clue; they show you are on the right track. If you are caught up playing in a Game Cube, Game stars will tell you how well you did.

Okay, that's all you need to know. Now
▶access page 1 - and good luck!

1

One fine, bright morning Bob feels a tingling under his skin. He looks up. The sky crackles, flickering with a bright circuitry glare one moment and blankness the next. The huge outline of a Game Cube is sliding down through the air.

Bob loses no time. Gunning his zipboard to full speed, he shoots in under the rim of the Game Cube before it reaches the ground.

"Okay," says Bob to the sprites who didn't manage to get clear. "What's the Game?" He looks around at the landscape, which just looks like a normal city street - though perhaps a bit run-down. Then three fighters advance out of the shadows.

"It's a martial arts thing," Bob realises. "REBOOT!"

Bob's normal costume is replaced by a wrestler's leotard. He has to pick one of the three opponents. Should he choose the karate ka (▶access page 10), the boxer (▶access page 28), or the judo expert (▶access page 19)?

2

Bob lashes out with his leg, but the karate ka reacts quickly. He blocks the kick with his forearm, steps in smartly and slams a terrific counterpunch into Bob's midriff.

"Ugh!" gasps Bob, and drops like a sack of potatoes.

The karate ka smiles almost apologetically as he bows to his fallen foe.

A klaxon sounds, announcing that play is proceeding to the next level. "I've got to be more careful, or I'm going to lose this one," resolves Bob grimly.

▶ access page 64.

3

The Sumotori swings an arm as thick as a tree branch. Bob can hear the whoosh as it sweeps over his head. Roll a die. If you get a score of 1-3, ▶access page 56. If you get 4-6, ▶access page 47.

4

Phong declares himself too busy to take any interest in new arrivals to the city.

"But these Knights Templates aren't just ordinary new arrivals," says Bob. "You ought to meet them."

"What is an 'ordinary' new arrival?" says Phong. "We hardly ever get visitors from the Super Computer."

Bob spreads his hands. "Exactly! So you'll meet them?"

"I'm afraid I'm far too busy with other matters, my son."

"How about a game of P.O.N.G.?"

Phong seems to be tempted, but after thinking about it for a little while, he shakes his head. "You always win, my son."

With a sigh, Bob gives up and decides to go and see Dot.

▶access page 75.

5

Dot calls up a vid-window to contact Bob. His face appears with a slightly harrassed expression. "Dot..." he says. "What's up?"

"I've got Null trouble over in business sector 12," says Dot.

A stool suddenly swings into view in the vid-window and crashes down across the back of Bob's head. He staggers, then turns round and punches someone who is out of Dot's range of vision. The vid-window changes position as Bob angles it to show Dot that he's having a major set-to with a gang of Megabyte's hoodlums.

"I'll get over there as soon as I can..." Bob gasps. The vid-window flashes out.

Roll a die. If you score 1-3, ▶access page 41. If you score 4 6, ▶access page 32.

6

Bob cannot help feeling slightly ill at ease as he skims through the air above the Gilded Gate Bridge and enters Lost Angles. It is not that he's afraid, but that the deserted alleys, chaotic street patterns and twisted perspectives make him feel as if he's going crazy.

He arrives at the vast underground amphitheatre where Hexadecimal is waiting like a brightly patterned spider in a web. It is thick with darkness. Bob slowly descends on his zipboard. "Hexadecimal," he says nervously. "Trick or treat!"

"Trick, I think," says a sinisterly seductive voice. All at once Bob is surrounded by flashing coloured lights in insane kaleidoscope patterns which threaten to tear his mind inside out.

What should he do? He could turn Glitch into a mirror (▶access page 52) or a pair of sunglasses (▶access page 61), or he could fly off on his zipboard while he still has the chance (▶access page 68).

7

Glitch becomes a small saw with a tungsten steel edge. But the metal of which the magnet is made is specially treated to make it stronger than a normal alloy.

Roll a die to see if Bob can think of something clever. If you score 1-3, he uses Glitch to cut through the wall he's pinned to: ▶access page 69. If you score 4 or more, he tries in vain to cut the magnet itself: ▶access page 25.

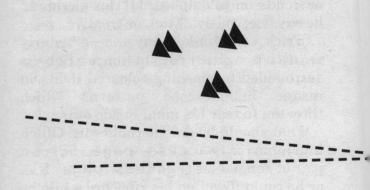

8

Bob returns to discover that Enzo is missing. "He was supposed to deliver some piezo-electric pizzas," says Dot, pointing to some boxes on the counter, "but he went out to get his zipboard and hasn't come back."

Bob rubs his jaw thoughtfully. "Well, you know Enzo..."

Dot is adamant. "Something's happened to him. I can't raise him by vid-window, for one thing."

What should Bob do? If he ought to search for Enzo on his own, ▶access page 18. If he ought to call in the Knights Templates to help him, ▶access page 36.

9

Bob tiptoes across the threshold and looks around. The interior is completely deserted. Still keeping as quiet as he can, he slips across to the back of the building and peers out into the alley running behind it. The Knights said they would be lying in wait there, but in fact they are nowhere to be seen.

"This really doesn't process," thinks Bob. "I'm getting back to the diner."

If you have the code ERSATZ, ▶access page 34. Otherwise, roll a die. If you score 1-3, ▶access page 71, and if you score 4-6, ▶access page 8.

10

No sooner has Bob made his choice than the man comes rushing forward, giving vent to a ferocious yell as he flails out with battle-hardened fists and feet.

If you think Bob should try a hip throw, ▶access page 73. If you think a kick would be more effective, ▶access page 2. If you think his best bet would be to wait for the karate ka to attack and then sidestep, ▶access page 55.

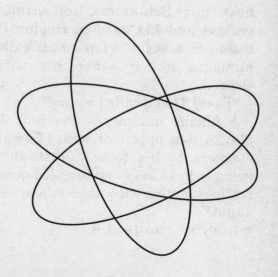

11

The boxer swings his jaw to one side just as Bob's fist comes up, so that the punch glides over its mark. "Neat trick!" says Bob, pausing to admire the fighter's technique.

The boxer cracks a smile for the first time, showing a quick flash of teeth as thin as a knife blade. "It's called shedding," he quips. "Want to see another good move?"

"Sure."

The boxer's fist lashes out in a blur. The next thing Bob knows, he's sitting on the ground and his head is ringing like the inside of a bell. "What's that called?" he manages to say when his wits have cleared.

"That? That's called losing!"

A klaxon announces the next level of play. A new opponent comes forward. Bob staggers to his feet, still stunned. "I'm going to have to get up to speed quickly," he realizes, "otherwise this whole sector is kaput!"

▶ access page 64.

12

Backing away, Bob slips Glitch off his wrist and lets him drop to the ground. The Sumotori doesn't notice - he has his beady gaze fixed firmly on his foe. As the Sumotori comes forward, shaking the ground with his stamping feet, Bob says simply, "Glitch - roller skate!"

A leg thicker than most people's waist comes down heavily on the roller skate that suddenly appears. The Sumotori yelps in surprise before his foot shoots out from under him. For an instant he is suspended in mid-air, like a barrage balloon wearing a jockstrap. Then he falls, sending seismic shockwaves through the ground. Bob feels his teeth rattling with the impact!

Bob retrieves Glitch. The Sumotori looks up, dazed and bewildered. "Who left that skate there?" he groans.

Bob whistles innocently. "Oh, some careless sprite, I guess."

The klaxon sounds again. It is time for the final contest.

▶ access page 74.

13

Bob scours the area using the energy-emission scanner built into Glitch, but he cannot find any sign of a Tear. "That's odd," he thinks. "The Game would have stabilized any Tear into a portal allowing access to the Super Computer. And when the Game vanished, the Tear should have destabilized again. I've never heard of a Tear repairing itself..."

Make a note of the code ERSATZ and then ▶ access page 75.

14

The next day another Game drops down to disrupt the lives of the citizens. The sky is criss-crossed with circuit board flashes and a warning voice intones, "Incoming Game. Incoming Game."

Bob looks around. "Residential sector 23. I'd better get a move on - there are an awful lot of sprites at risk there."

Just then there's a cry for help from the street below. Bob glances down to see a bunch of viral binomes who have forced a bus off the road and are threatening the passengers with stunsticks. Bob cannot ignore their plight. He must deal with the hoodlums fast though, otherwise he will be too late to reach the Game and save the sprites of residential sector 23.

What should he do? He could catch the hoodlums by using Glitch (▶access page 15) or his zipboard (▶access page 24). Or he could wait until the hoodlums make their getaway and then follow them to their hideout (▶access page 33).

15

Bob uses Glitch as a net to catch the crooks. But since he then has to carry the hoodlums to the city penitentiary he has to miss the Game. "I hope the User didn't win," he frets to himself. "Otherwise a whole sector will have been off-lined."

▶ access page 42.

16

What were you or Bob thinking of? You can't use a lockpick on a magnet - the magnetic field doesn't have a lock to pick!
▶ access page 25.

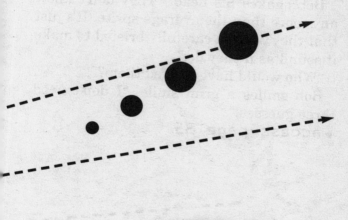

17

Bob is sure of one thing - the Knights Templates are not from the Super Computer.

"But they seem to know quite a bit about it," says Dot, when Bob tells her his suspicions.

Bob shakes his head. "They don't know any more than the average sprite. It's just that they've been carefully briefed to make it sound as if they do."

"Who would have briefed them?"

Bob smiles a grim smile. "I don't need three guesses!"

▶ access page 35.

18

Bob and Dot follow Enzo's trail.

"I saw it all," says a sprite hanging around on the street corner selling news print-outs.

"What happened?" Bob asks him.

"Hack and Slash grabbed Enzo. See, there's his baseball cap."

Dot picks up the cap from the pavement. "It's Enzo's alright," she sighs. "I can guess where they've taken him."

The sprite points. "To the top of Silicon Tor! The penthouse suite, I guess you'd have to call it."

▶ access page 27.

19

The judo expert is a broad-shouldered man with stocky limbs. He advances towards Bob in a square-on stance, with his arms open wide as if ready to give Bob a hug.

"Are we fighting or dancing?" asks Bob.

"Hey," says the judo expert with a confident smile, "you tell me. You're the one with the silver mop on his head."

What should Bob do? If you think he should try and grapple his opponent head-on, ▶access page 37. If he ought to throw a punch, ▶access page 46. If he'd be better off going for a leg sweep to knock the man over, ▶access page 55.

20

Bob gets a tight hold on the boxer, who pushes him back against a fence which lines the side of the road. They end up in a clinch. The boxer grinds his forehead against Bob's chin.

"Ow!" says Bob. "I thought there were rules to boxing?"

"There are," hisses the boxer under his breath. "The first rule is: Don't get caught when you cheat!"

Bob is taking a pummelling. Should he use Glitch to get an advantage (▶access page 29), or break out of the clinch and try either a right cross (▶access page 55) or a left jab (▶access page 11)?

21

Bob isn't one to be dismayed just because he's facing an opponent twice as big as he is. But unfortunately reckless courage isn't always enough. He goes charging in, fists swinging - and runs smack into one of the User's sledgehammer punches. One blow is all that's needed. Bob drops in his tracks with a groan. What makes defeat even harder to bear is the knowledge that this whole sector will now go off-line, turning into a dark chasm in the middle of the city, its former population reduced to mindless Nulls...

▶ access page 48.

22

Enzo notices that the Knights all have some kind of machine code symbol on their breastplates. Also, although they have zipboards, they only have one between two of them.

Enzo knows that the Knights will get bored of answering too many questions, so he'd better pick his questions carefully. If you think he should ask about the symbol, ▶access page 40. If you're more intrigued by the zipboards, ▶access page 49. If he ought to ask more about where the knights come from, ▶access page 58.

23

Dot dashes into the warehouse and slams the metal door down. She can hear the Nulls crash against it like damp fireworks.

She piles some crates together and stands on them, to look out of an upper window. To her great relief, the Knights Templates have arrived on the scene. However, she's baffled by what they're saying to each other.

"Is she here?" says one of the Knights, peering down from the vantage point of his zipboard at the tide of Nulls.

"She must have got away," replies another.

"Or been deleted by the Nulls," adds a Knight.

"What shall we do about them?" asks one.

"Leave them," decides the chief Knight. "They've done their job."

They streak away across the rooftops. Bewildered Dot waits until the Nulls have dispersed before venturing outside.

▶ access page 50.

24

Bob lands on the cornice of a building and lobs his zipboard like a discus. It slams into the hoodlums, knocking them to the ground. Seeing they are stunned, Bob catches his zipboard and heads off in the direction of the Game Cube. He might just get there in time -

"Ooof!"

Bob slams into two of the Knights Templates who drop from the flight lane just above him without signalling. All three tumble to the ground. As Bob comes to, he looks up and gives a groan of dismay. The Game Cube has landed, and he's trapped outside.

Bob can hardly contain his frustration and anger. "Sorry, you say? Don't you know you might have doomed all the sprites caught inside the Cube?"

"Don't worry," says one of the Knights. "Our comrades are dealing with it right now."

Make a note of the code FORTRESS and then ▶ access page 42.

25

Bob is well and truly trapped. All he can do is wait until Megabyte returns to deal with him. Whatever fate Megabyte has in store for him, he can be sure it won't be a pleasant one. Erasure by magnetic field, perhaps? Or murder by psychotic delete-command sprites? Or perhaps having all his energy sucked out of him by vampiric Nulls?

Rather than dwell on Bob's cruel fate, get ready to try again. Cross off any access codes and Game stars you scored this time and ▶ access page 1.

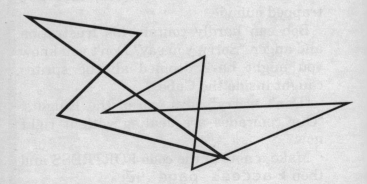

26

Bob walks into the diner shaking his head. "That code symbol on the Knights' armour..." he says.

"What about it?" asks Dot.

"It's too primitive to be part of a Super Computer program," says Bob. "I should have realized it before!"

"They aren't from the Super Computer, then?"

"I'm beginning to have my suspicions," mutters Bob.

▶access page 35.

27

As Bob and Dot come rush into the lobby of Silicon Tor, they are immediately confronted by Hack and Slash.

"Sorry," says one.

"Closed," says the other.

Bob sets his jaw grimly. "Out of our way, bozos. We've come for Enzo."

"You're going to have to get past him and me," says Slash... or Hack, maybe? The red one, anyhow.

"Get past me and him, that's right," says the blue one.

If you have the access code MONOPOLE, ▶access page 45. Otherwise, decide whether Bob and Dot should tackle Hack and Slash together (▶access page 54), or whether Dot should keep them busy while Bob goes off to find Enzo (▶access page 63)?

28

The boxer closes in at a rapid trot, weaving left and right behind his huge fists.

Bob's first couple of punches both hit nothing but empty air. "Keep still, can't you?" he protests. "How can I land a punch if you keep ducking about like that?"

The boxer says nothing. His face is a mask of cold concentration. Bob can sense him getting ready to deliver a devastating blow.

It's up to you to decide Bob's best tactics. Should he go for a left jab (▶access page 11), an arm lock (▶access page 20), or a drop kick (▶access page 55)?

29

Bob turns Glitch into a baton, which he uses to prod the boxer away. Before he can launch a fresh attack, a klaxon sounds and a little man in baggy trousers rushes up. "That's against the rules," says the man. "You're disqualified."

"Who are you?" asks Bob.

"I'm the referee."

"But, ref - he cheated first!" says Bob, pointing at the boxer. "He headbutted me!"

The boxer grins. "I told you, matey-boy. Don't get caught."

The referee looks at Bob. "Get ready for the next bout. And I don't want to have to tell you again - no cheating!"

"Or at least, if you must cheat, do it discreetly," whispers the boxer as the next opponent arrives on the scene.

▶access page 64.

30

Bob backs away until he is under the awning of a shopfront. He glances back at the shop doorway, but a glowing message written there reads: CONTESTANTS WHO LEAVE THE STREET ARE DISQUALIFIED.

"Huh, typical!" thinks Bob. "I expect the Game designer couldn't be bothered to program in the graphics for indoor fighting."

The User is closing in with long menacing strides. Should Bob surprise him with a sudden attack (▶access page 21) or swing himself up onto the awning to get a height advantage(▶access page 27)?

31

Enzo flies his zipboard over to the mall, where his friends are hanging out by the vid-window arcade. They are amazed to hear his news.

"New guys in Mainframe!" gasps a sprite called Ed. "That doesn't happen very often."

"Not just ordinary newcomers, either," says Enzo. "They're all tooled up like knights in a dungeon Game."

"I wonder what they're here for?" says another of his friends.

"To play Games, of course!" says Enzo. "What else?"

If you want to stick around with Enzo, ▶access page 76. If you want to see what Dot is doing, ▶access page 67. If you'd rather check in on Bob, ▶access page 14.

32

A shadow makes Dot look up. It is a dozen or so of the Knights Templates on their old-fashioned zipboards. Dot can't remember the last time she was so relieved to see anyone.

"Do not panic, Miss," says one of the Knights. "We will use our energy lances to stampede these Nulls back where they came from."

"Thanks," Dot calls back, as she watches them herd the Nulls in the direction of the Gilded Gate Bridge. "And by the way, it's 'Ms', not 'Miss'."

▶ access page 50.

33

The hoodlums lead Bob straight back to Silicon Tor, Megabyte's cobra-hooded skyscraper. "Of course," mutters Bob to himself. "Where else? Megabyte's behind every misdemeanour in Mainframe."

He glides under a projecting cornice and watches the doors, but no one comes out of the tower. By now it is too late to get involved in the Game, but Bob cannot help wondering how the trapped sprites fared without his help.

Should he go back to check on the Game? If you think so, ▶access page 69. Otherwise he might try sneaking into Megabyte's lair (▶access page 51). Or he could just march in openly (▶access page 60).

34

Bob is starting to get very suspicious about the so-called Knights Templates. There are things about them that don't quite add up. Each clue on its own wouldn't amount to much, but all in all they are starting to add up to give a very sinister picture.

Check your access codes. If you have FORTRESS, ▶access page 17. If you have INSIGNIA, ▶access page 26. If you don't have either code, ▶access page 8.

35

Enzo puts through a vid-window call to tell Bob and Dot that he's onto something. "Frisket's picked up someone's scent!" he says excitedly.

"So?" says Bob, unable to see what the fuss is about.

Dot's eyes light up. "Don't you remember?" she says. "Frisket sniffed the Knights' cloaks when they were here."

"And now he can lead us to their headquarters!" says Bob. "We'll be right with you, Enzo."

Frisket follows the scent trail directly to Silicon Tor - the high, brooding tower of Megabyte's lair.

"Well," says Dot, "now we know who's behind the Knights Templates."

Bob takes his zipboard up to the top of the tower and peers in through a skylight. In the room below, confirming his suspicions, he sees the Knights Templates receiving orders from Megabyte - their master!

▶ access page 72.

36

The Knights scour the city. Soon their leader comes with good news. "We have tracked down the gang who kidnapped Enzo," he tells Bob.

Bob follows them on his zipboard to a derelict building on the lowest level. "He's in there," say the Knights.

Half out of his mind with worry, Bob charges straight into the building without a thought for his own safety. Unfortunately.

▶ access page 71.

37

Bob's opponent grabs his arm, gives it a powerful wrench, and Bob is flipped over onto his back before he even knows what's going on. "Oooff!" he grunts as the wind is knocked out of him. "We'll call it the best of three falls, shall we?"

"Sorry," says his opponent, shaking his head. "One fall is all you're allowed. We're going on to level two now - you'd better get with the program or quit file."

"Huh!" snorts Bob, leaping to his feet. "I'm just getting warmed up."

▶ access page 64.

38

As the Game Cube sputters and fades, Bob notices a group of strange figures with silver armour, swords and long white cloaks lingering at the perimeter of the Game zone.

They bow politely. "We are the Knights Templates. We regret we arrived too late to assist you in the Game."

"Arrived?" says Bob. "Arrived from where?"

"From the Super Computer. We are guardian programs like yourself. We came through a Tear that the Game stabilized to allow transit."

Bob's eyes narrow. He hides his suspicion with a smile.

The Knights raise their swords in a military salute. "We are here to protect the weak, and chastise the wicked!"

Should Bob take the Knights to meet Dot (▶access page 75), introduce them to Phong (▶access page 4), or spend some time looking for the Tear they mentioned (▶access page 13)?

39

The User looms closer, raising a titanic fist against the sky. Bob stands stock-still, timing his move to the last nanosecond.

The User swings with all his strength. Bob jumps aside. The User's fist smashes through the brickwork where Bob had been standing just a moment before, and the User gives a snarl of frustrated rage as half the wall collapses, trapping his fist.

Bob seizes his chance. While his opponent is struggling to pull his fist out of the debris, Bob jumps forward and unleases a barrage of blows straight into the mask-like face. The User sways and is sent crashing to the ground. The crowd cheer delightedly to see their hero triumph yet again.

The Game is over. Award yourself a final Game star and then ▶access page 48.

Make a note of the access code INSIGNIA.

One of the Knights points proudly to the symbol etched into his metal armour. "This is the primary code of our Order. We call it the chivalric code. It represents the complex oaths of honour, courage, discipline and humility that each of us must take in order to become one of the Knights Templates."

"It doesn't sound very easy to join," says Enzo.

"Indeed it is not," declares another Knight firmly. "Anyone who wants to join must be totally dedicated to our cause."

"Now, excuse us," says another Knight. "We must patrol the city in case our services are needed."

Enzo watches them file out of the diner. True to form, he is already toying with the idea that one day he might qualify for knighthood.

▶ access page 67.

41

The delay costs Dot her chance to get away. The Nulls fall on her like a swarm of angry wasps - except that wasps only sting a person. Nulls suck out all the energy so that all that's left is an empty husk.

Poor Dot. You failed this time, but you can always try again. Just cross off any access codes and Game stars you scored this time, then REBOOT at `page 1`.

42

A dozen of the Knights Templates manage to enter the Game just before it touches the ground. The Knights team up heroically to defeat the User in a contest involving tanks, fighter planes and ground-to-air missiles.

The sprites who are trapped inside have never seen anything like it. "Three cheers for the Knights Templates!" cry the delighted citizens as the Game Cube begins to fade.

"They're pretty cool," says Enzo, who has seen the Knights in action. "But I wonder how Bob feels about the arrival of a new bunch of Game champions in Mainframe?"

A sprite standing nearby overhears this and says, "Bob didn't get to this Game in time, did he? If you ask me, these Knights Templates are much better. After all, Bob can't be everywhere at once."

Enzo thinks that's unfair. It is very rare for Bob to fail to reach a Game.

▶access page 69.

43

Check the list of access codes you've managed to acquire.

If you have FORTRESS and/or INSIGNIA, ▶access page 78.

If you don't have either code, ▶access page 68.

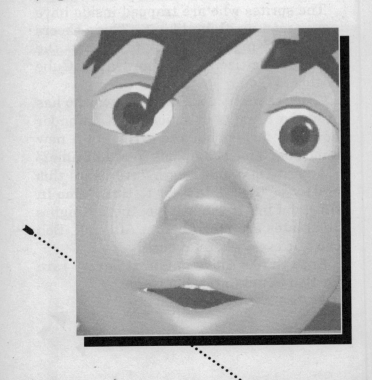

44

Bob and Dot are talking about something very intently, so Enzo decides to take Frisket for a walk. After a few blocks Frisket starts sniffing the ground, then bounds along to the next corner.

"You're following someone's trail, aren't you?" says Enzo. "Maybe it's important!"

What do you think? If Enzo should fetch Bob, ▶access page 35. If he should first see where the trail leads to, ▶access page 62.

45

Bob activates the Null attractor and hands it to Hack. "Here's a present," he says.

"What is it?" asks Hack warily.

Bob tells him. "Any second now you'll have a swarm of Nulls after you."

Hack tosses the attractor to Slash. "Here, you have it!"

Slash tosses it back. "No, you!"

They both go racing off down the street, throwing the attractor back and forth like a potato straight out of the oven, pursued by a buzzing wave of Nulls.

"Dimwits!" laughs Dot. "They don't think to just drop the attractor."

"It's even worse than that," says Bob, grinning. "They're robots - the Nulls can't hurt them anyway!"

Searching the basement, they find the cell where Enzo is being held and soon have him free.

▶access page 72.

46

Bob swings his fist in a powerful uppercut. It is the kind of punch that could make even Megabyte's head spin - if it hits its mark, that is!

Roll a die to see if Bob's opponent sees it coming. If you score 1-3, ▶access page 37. If you score 4-6, ▶access page 55.

47

The Sumotori gives a great thunderclap yell as he slams into Bob - one hundred and fifty kilos of bone and blubber with a bad attitude. It's like being slapped in the face with a sperm whale. Bob rebounds off him, reels back into a wall, and goes down. The onlookers give a dismayed moan. "Bob!" they cry. "You've got to fight back or we'll all be turned into Nulls!"

The klaxon sounds again, and a deep voice declares, "The final level..."

▶ access page 74.

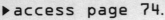

48

Did you score any stars during the Game? If you scored three Game stars, you count as a Champion fighter. If you scored two Game stars, consider yourself a Master of the martial arts. If you scored one, you are an Expert. If you didn't get any Game stars then you're only a Novice - but you'll know better next time.

Now ▶access page 38.

49

Enzo remarks on how they only have one zipboard for every two Knights.

"This is to remind us of the need for modesty, which is one of the primary virtues of knighthood," explains one of them.

"Er, sure," says Enzo, "but doesn't it get crowded with two of you on one board?"

"Of course. It is a constant reminder that we are all members of a team, and each Knight must rely on his brethren."

"There is no more time for talk," says another of the Knights. "We should go on patrol in case our services are needed."

Enzo watches them file out of the diner. Being the keen young copy.com sprite he is, Enzo is already wondering what it would be like to be a Knight.

▶ access page 67.

50

Dot meets up with Enzo and Bob that afternoon at the zipboard rink. As they glide and soar around the inside of the spherical rink, Dot wonders how much she should say about the Null attack earlier today. If she gives all the details then Bob will know how close she came to being deleted. But if she doesn't tell him then he can't help her solve the mystery of why Nulls should be prowling the streets in such numbers.

What do you think? Should she tell him (▶access page 59), or let the matter drop (▶access page 68)?

51

Make a note of the access code FORTRESS.

Bob takes the zipboard up to maximum altitude and hovers outside the top of Silicon Tor. The windows are shaped like a cobra's eyes. Inside, he can see Megabyte's tall, jutting silhouette as he discusses his plans with his henchman. Where Megabyte is concerned, 'discussion' just involves an endless self-satisfied rant, so Bob has no trouble overhearing what he is saying.

"They're taking everyone in," comes the sinister, feline purr of Megabyte's voice. "Even the brat thinks they're heroes. Once they have everyone's trust, I shall be poised to - Wait! What's that outside the window?"

What should Bob do - fly off (▶access page 69) or stay and confront his arch-foe (▶access page 60)?

52

Bob puts the mirror across his eyes, tilting it so the hypnotic lights reflect back at Hexadecimal herself. "Ah, the chaotic colours..." she murmurs admiringly.

Bob can hardly believe his luck - she is in a trance! "What can you tell me about the Nulls that attacked Dot?" he asks.

Hexadecimal answers dreamily, "The Nulls left Lost Angles this morning and came back a few hours later."

"They left for no reason? Didn't that bother you?" Bob questions.

Hexadecimal's face becomes a frowning mask. "Bother me? Of course not. I approve of senseless actions..."

"What about the attack on Dot? You weren't behind that?" probes Bob.

"I don't know about any attack..." Hexadecimal sighs.

Should Bob look for clues at the scene of the Nulls' attack (▶access page 77), should he question Hexadecimal further (▶access page 70), or rejoin Dot and Enzo (▶access page 68)?

53

It is no easy matter to move Frisket when Frisket doesn't want to be moved. In fact, Enzo is reminded about the Sumo wrestler from the Game Bob played earlier. After much shoving, tugging and jabbing, he manages to convince Frisket to go outside.

The Knights collect their cloaks and file out to get on their zipboards.

"Are you leaving?" says Enzo, disappointed because he didn't get to ask them about the Super Computer.

"We must," replies one of the Knights. "It is our sworn duty to patrol the city and protect the honest citizens from crime and disaster. But we shall return."

So saying, they zip off into the sky.

▶ access page 67.

54

Bob and Dot together are no match for the mechanical strength of Hack and Slash. They are soon caught fast and taken up in the elevator to face Megabyte.

"We should have tried to outwit them," realizes Bob, too late.

Bob, Dot and Enzo are all Megabyte's prisoners! Things can't get much worse...

The only thing for it now is to try again from the start. Cross off any access codes and Game stars you scored this time, then REBOOT at page 1.

55

Bob's opponent is floored. The watching sprites raise a happy cheer. To them this is much more than a Game. Unless Bob wins, this whole sector will go off-line, leaving just a gaping abyss between the surrounding buildings.

Award yourself one Game star. (Keep a running tally of these on the adventure notes pages at the back of the book, to show how well you're doing.)

When you're ready for the next stage of the Game, ▶ access page 64.

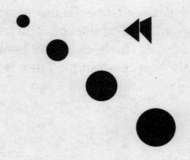

56

Bob leaps aside as the Sumotori comes thudding forward with outstretched arms. Bob catches the back of his belt, shoves with all his strength, and the giant Sumotori goes staggering. There is no way the Sumotori can stop himself - he's built up more momentum than a falling redwood. Bob watches as he crashes through a doorway, reducing it to splinters the size of matches. The Sumotori topples to the ground.

"The bigger they come, the harder they fall," says Bob, brushing his hands. "Next, please!"

Award yourself one Game star. (Keep a running tally of these on the adventure notes pages at the back of the book to show how well you're doing.) Then ▶ access page 74.

57

Bob flips up onto the awning and uses it like a trampoline to somersault over the User's head. His plan is to strike from behind, before the User can see where he's got to. But such a desperate ploy must contain an element of risk, so roll a die. If you score 1-3, ▶access page 66. If you score 4-6, ▶access page 21.

58

Make a note of the access code FORTRESS.

"We are from the Super Computer," the Knights tell him.

"Really?" says Enzo. "Bob too! Hey, Bob, did you know any of the Knights while you were in the Super Computer?"

"No, I can't say that I did..." Bob murmurs thoughtfully. "Which files were you guys guarding?"

"It is a matter of restricted access," replies a Knight instantly.

Bob sips his coffee. "How about the class of portal you came through?"

The nearest Knight gives him a narrow-eyed look. "It was a stabilized Tear."

"Yeah, but was it Class Three, Class Four, or what?"

The Knights look at each other, then get up. "This has been pleasant," says one, abruptly. "We will talk again when there is more time. Now we must patrol the city."

Enzo and Bob watch them leave. Bob is deep in thought.

▶ access page 67.

59

"It's really odd," says Bob. "You sometimes get one or two Nulls drifting about eating up energy traces, but - "

"But it's rare to get a whole swarm of them outside Lost Angles," says Dot. "I know. I wondered if Hexadecimal was behind it?"

"Maybe," replies Bob. "Her control over the Nulls extends long range. But could she direct them from her island, once they've left Lost Angles?"

Dot pats him on the shoulder. "Keep working on it, Bob. I'm confident you'll solve the mystery for me."

Bob is so pleased at Dot's praise that he hardly notices how she's managed to get him to do exactly what she wants yet again.

What do you suggest Bob should do now - take a look at the warehouse where the Nulls attacked (▶access page 77), drop in on Hexadecimal (▶access page 6), or wait to see what develops (▶access page 68)?

60

"Bob!" says Megabyte, pretending to be pleased to see him. "Do stick around." He snaps his fingers and a large magnet shoots out of a slot in the wall. The magnet knocks back against a steel door and pins Bob there as if he'd been stapled.

"You can see the attraction of having a magnet around, can't you?" says Megabyte. "Now, I have to leave you for a while, since I have other matters to attend to. Oh, and Bob - " Megabyte pauses at the door.

"Yes?" gasps Bob.

"Mind you don't touch the poles." Megabyte chuckles and leaves the room.

Bob doesn't need to be reminded not to touch the poles of the magnet - the magnetic field would erase him like a floppy disk. But he can't stay trapped while Megabyte cooks up an evil scheme.

It is safe for Glitch to touch the magnet. Should Bob get Glitch to turn into a blowtorch (▶access page 80), a saw (▶access page 7), or alternatively a lockpick (▶access page 16)?

61

Bob slips on the sunglasses. Now that the hypnotic lights are screened out he feels much better. He also looks really cool.

Hexadecimal glides over to his side. "Bob, I'm wounded! Don't you like my little light show?"

"It's mesmerizing," says Bob, "but I've got other things on my mind right now. Like, what caused a swarm of Nulls to attack Dot this morning?"

"Poor Dot! Sucked dry of her life force; no more energy in her than a spent battery."

"Dot's fine," says Bob. "She got away from the Nulls."

Hexadecimal gives a scornful sniff. "Oh, too bad. Well, it's nothing to do with me, anyway. I prefer to let the Nulls have their own way most of the time."

"Even if you had commanded the Nulls to attack Dot, would you tell me?" Bob wonders as he gets back on his zipboard.

"Probably not," smiles Hexadecimal sweetly, watching him fly off.

▶ access page 68.

62

Frisket pulls Enzo all the way to Silicon Tor. "Hey! Megabyte's headquarters!" says Enzo. "But if the Knights Templates are here, that means they're working for - "

"Who?" interrupts two gruff voices behind him.

Enzo whirls. It is Hack and Slash, Megabyte's robot henchmen. Enzo goes to run, but each of them grabs an arm. Frisket growls angrily, but before he can leap, Hack and Slash have hovered up out of reach. Enzo is held dangling high above the ground.

"Megabyte says, nice of you..."

"...nice of you to drop by."

"He says that."

"I said it."

"He said it, but Megabyte says it too."

"Great!" sighs Enzo. "Not only did I get myself caught, but I got myself caught by a pair of morons!"

Frisket bounds off. He means to bring Bob and Dot to the rescue.

▶ access page 27.

63

Dot steps between the two robots. "I don't know which of you is more stupid," she says. "Your heads are just stuffed with wingnuts."

"Hey!" says Slash, raising his huge fist.

"That's rude!" says Hack, winding up a bolo punch.

They charge just as Dot backpedals. Hack and Slash are too slow to stop themselves. Each gives the other a powerful clout. The sound is like two church bells colliding at ninety miles an hour.

"Owww..." moans part of the debris when the dust has settled.

"Oooh..." agrees another scrap of metal lying nearby.

Dot shakes her head. "What did I tell you?" she retorts, before hurrying to catch up with Bob, who has already found and freed Enzo.

▶ access page 72.

64

Bob's next opponent is a huge Sumo wrestler. "He looks like he eats a couple of kilobytes for breakfast each day!" thinks Bob in alarm. "If he sits on me I'm going to be left as flat as he is fat."

The Sumotori stamps his way forward, his huge belly quaking with every step. With a sneer, he tosses a fistful of salt on the ground.

"What's that for?" asks Bob.

"Soaks up the blood," replies the Sumotori.

"Ulp!" says Bob, not sure if he's joking or not.

The Sumotori gives a sudden roar and lifts his arms. He looks like he might be about to charge. Should Bob dodge in under his arms and attempt to throw him (▶access page 47), sidestep quickly (▶access page 56), or try a body punch (▶access page 65)?

65

Bob's fist whacks into the huge Sumotori's belly - to no effect. Under all that flab there is yet more flab, as well as some huge slabs of muscle. Bob might as well try punching a mattress.

"Hah!" laughs the Sumotori. "I think I felt a gnat sting me!"

What now? Should Bob attempt a throw (▶access page 47), a dodge (▶access page 3), or use Glitch to win the bout (▶access page 12)?

66

Bob lands like a cat, twisting his body into an agile leap that carries him onto the User's back. He claps his hands hard on either side of his enemy's head, causing the User to give a grunt of annoyance and swing one of his heavy fists back over his head to try and dislodge him. This is exactly what Bob was counting on - he grabs the User's arm and adds his own weight to the blow, swinging the fist into the back of the User's own head. It hits with the force of a wrecking ball, and the User is left staggering. Bob completes the job with a leg sweep that brings the User to the ground.

The Game is over. Award yourself a Game star and then ▶access page 48.

67

The next day, Dot drops in at one of her warehouses to collect some vehicle parts that have been ordered through a shipping company she owns - just one of Dot's many business interests around Mainframe. As she is telling the binomes who work at the warehouse which crates she needs, one of them gives a peep of alarm and points down the street.

Dot turns, seeing nothing at first. She then squints, and makes out a wave of glittering worm-like things flowing towards her. It is a horde of Nulls.

"Run," yells Dot to her employees. She knows that the Nulls can leech away the life-energy of living sprites.

If Dot should run too, ▶access page 32. If she should call for help, ▶access page 5. But if she should hide inside the warehouse, ▶access page 23.

68

The Knights Templates find Bob at the diner. "We need your help," they tell him.

"How can I refuse?" grins Bob. "Help to do what, exactly?"

"We've tracked a gang of criminals to their base on the lowest level. Your knowledge of the city would be invaluable in rounding them up."

Bob cannot resist any opportunity for action, and the Knights' flattery is just the icing on the cake. He follows them to a gloomy area of the city.

The Knights indicate a shop with shuttered windows covered in digital graffiti. "They're in there. We'll go round the back. You wait until we're ready, then charge in the front way. The criminals will come out the back and we'll grab them."

The Knights leave Bob at the front of the building. Should he rush in without warning (▶access page 71), yell to tell the criminals he's coming (▶access page 79), or sneak in quietly (▶access page 9)?

69

Enzo runs to Bob the moment the Game Cube fades. "It was fantastic! The Knights showed up and there were jet planes and missiles with warheads and stuff and they just trashed the lot. The User had a big gunship and they turned it into scrap ."

Bob frowns. Something is bothering him - and he hopes it isn't just jealousy.

When they arrive back at the diner Dot tells them she was attacked by Nulls outside one of her warehouses. "There was a big swarm of them, but guess what..?"

"The Knights Templates came to your rescue?" says Bob.

"That's right!" says Dot. "How did you guess?"

Bob thinks it's odd that Nulls have been streaming around outside Lost Angles. Should he go to investigate Dot's warehouse (▶access page 77), drop in on Hexadecimal (▶access page 6) or wait for more clues to come his way before taking any action (▶access page 68)?

70

Bob has waited around too long, and now Hexadecimal has shrugged off the hypnotic trance she was in. "Bob, I feel humiliated. That really wasn't very nice of you."

"The hypnosis was your own idea. I just turned the tables on you."

Hexadecimal sighs. "Oh, I suppose I was in the wrong."

Her tone makes Bob uneasy. "So we're quits?"

"No, no!" protests Hexadecimal. "I was wrong to try and hypnotize you. You'll have to stay until I can think of a way to atone for my bad manners..."

With a gesture, she turns the floor under Bob's feet into a vat of quick-setting cement. He has no chance to move before he is sucked down and trapped like a bug in amber.

There's little hope for Mainframe with Bob out of the way. You failed this time, but you can always try again. Just cross off any access codes and Game stars you scored this time, then REBOOT at page 1.

71

Bob steps across the threshold. He feels a tug at his ankle and, glancing down, sees a tripwire.

"Tab it!..." he has time to say. Then a bomb explodes into a blaze of flaming debris.

Bob has been well and truly deleted. You failed this time, but try again and you might be able to find out who planted that bomb. Maybe you have your suspicions already? To start again, just cross off any access codes and Game stars you scored this time, then REBOOT at page 1.

High up in Silicon Tor, Megabyte gives his orders to the Knights Templates - unaware that Bob is recording him using Glitch.

"The citizens of Mainframe are so gullible!" he is saying. "They really believe you're from the Super Computer."

"Indeed they do, my lord...er...that is... I mean boss," says one of the 'Knights'. It is now plain to see that they are just typical sprites from one of Megabyte's low-life gangs, disguised in metal armour.

Megabyte smacks his fist into his hand. "Excellent!" he roars. "When I have their trust it will be all the easier to corrupt them. Already they are beginning to lose their unwavering confidence in Bob and turn to you, my Knights, as their new champions."

"After seeing this vid-data I've got?" says Bob to himself with a smile as he slips away. "I don't think so!"

▶ access page 81.

73

Bob turns side-on to his opponent and jumps forward, pressing his hip into the man's side and pivoting him over.

"Hey!" yelps the opponent. "What - ?"

"It's called leverage," explains Bob. "Archimedes said that with a big enough lever you could lift the world. Luckily all I need to lift is you."

Roll a die. If you score 1-3, ▶access page 37. If you score 4 6, ▶access page 55.

74

Bob's third and last opponent is the User himself. He appears in the Game as a towering giant, with fists like rock hammers. As usual, the User's face is just a blank iconic mask.

What should Bob do? He is outmatched in reach and strength, and the User doesn't look slow for his size either. Should Bob go for a direct attack (▶ access page 21), retreat and think of a plan (▶ access page 30), or stand against a wall and wait for the User to strike (▶ access page 39)?

75

The Knights Templates crowd into Dot's Diner, filling all the available tables. "I've seen some strange customers in my time," says Dot with a smile, "but knights in armour? Where did you find them?"

Bob tells her. "If they're halfway-decent guardians, they'll be a real help. We needn't lose a Game to the User ever again."

The Knights have hung their cloaks inside the door. Dot notices that Frisket has gone over to sniff the shiny white fabric. "Enzo!" she yells. "What's wrong with Frisket? He never comes into the diner. Please put him out."

Enzo wants to talk to the Knights and see what adventures they've had. Should he deal with Frisket right away (▶access page 53), ask the Knights a few questions before they leave (▶ access page 22), or go and tell his friends about the new arrivals in town (▶ access page 31)?

76

The next day, Enzo is gliding aimlessly on his zipboard across the upper levels of the city when there is a crackling sound. The sky blips like a vid-screen with a faulty circuit. "Game!" cries Enzo. "And I'm right under it. Alphanumeric!"

He directs his zipboard down, spiralling in under the edge of the descending Game Cube as it slides inexorably down out of the sky.

▶ access page 42.

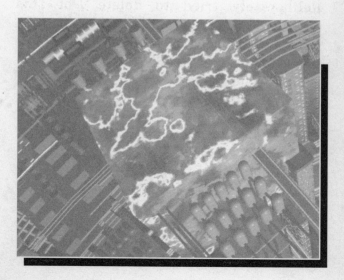

77

Make a note of the access code MONOPOLE.

Bob goes over to the warehouse and takes a look around. With Glitch's help he has soon discovered something hidden behind a stack of crates. It looks like an aerial with a power pack attached. When Bob studies it through Glitch's scanning screen, he makes an alarming discovery: "It's set to give off energy at the exact frequency that attracts Nulls! Someone deliberately tried to delete Dot this morning!"

Look at your access codes. If ERSATZ is one of them, ▶access page 34. If not, ▶access page 43.

78

There is something niggling at the back of Bob's mind, but he can't quite put his finger on it. He resolves to stay alert - if anything untoward is going to happen, he means to be ready to deal with it.

▶ access page 44.

79

Bob cups his hands to his mouth and yells, "Hey, you in there! Get ready, I'm coming in!"

There is no reply. Bob peers into the darkened building. "That's odd," he thinks. He had expected a snarl of defiance at the very least.

Should he run inside (▶access page 71), sneak in quietly (▶access page 9), or give up and make his way back to the diner (▶access page 8)?

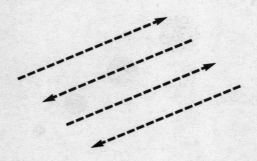

80

Perhaps you know, as Bob does, that heat destroys a magnet's attraction. The magnet slips away and falls to the floor - now just a harmless hoop of iron.

"I'd better be getting back to check on that Game Cube," decides Bob, jumping onto his zipboard. "Too bad I can't stick around to see the look on Megabyte's face when he finds I've got free of his dastardly magnet trap!"

He flies off in the direction of the Game.

▶ access page 69.

81

Bob broadcasts his data by vid-window across all of Mainframe. As soon as the citizens realize they've been duped, an angry crowd gathers outside Silicon Tor and the so-called 'knights' are forced to flee for their lives.

Relaxing in the diner, Bob and Dot are surprised to get a vid-window call from Megabyte himself. They can tell right away from his carefully polite tone that he is very angry. "Sneaking in and spying on me wasn't very sporting of you, Bob."

"Maybe," agrees Bob. "Not much more sporting than dressing up a bunch of thugs as knights and leading everyone in Mainframe into relying on them."

Megabyte simmers for a moment. "I'll get even with you Bob, never fear."

The vid-window goes blank. "Wow, Megabreath sounded really annoyed with you Bob," says Enzo.

Bob smiles and puts his feet up, totally unconcerned. "Don't worry, he'll get over it," he says. "He's just had a bad Knight!"

Access Codes

DATA RECORD
Access Codes

DATA RECORD
Access Codes

Access Codes

DATA RECORD
Game Stars

DATA RECORD
Game Stars

DATA RECORD
Game Stars

-- -- -- -- -- -- -- -- -- --

DATA RECORD
Game Stars

Have you read these other exciting ReBoot Adventure Game Books?

- Virtual Life

- The Virus Hunter

- Racing the Clock